Active Comprehension

Book 2

Margaret Stillie
and
Richard Hegarty

STANLEY THORNES

Stanley Thornes (Publishers) Ltd

Notes for Teachers

Active Comprehension is a structured four book course for children aged 7-11 that links comprehension to core reading and writing skills and across the whole primary curriculum. It develops comprehension through lively activities and complete cross-curricular topics.

The higher order skills involved in reading and writing are central to all the activities that the children will be engaged in. These skills will be applied to English and to other areas of the curriculum such as Science, History, Geography, Religious Education, Technology and Information Technology, through the use of good-quality fiction, poetry and different forms of non-fiction.

Active Comprehension:
- allows children to work independently;
- exercises comprehension skills beyond the literal and reorganisational levels, and encourages the development of positive attitudes to reading;
- gives children purposes for writing and support as writers in a context relevant to their age and experience;
- encourages children to use appropriate language in relation to written English;
- emphasises the development of accuracy in spelling and punctuation;
- incorporates Levels 2-5 of the National Curriculum in relation to skills and content.

Children will encounter the following symbols throughout the series. These symbols are designed to encourage further skills development:

Use the library

Use a computer

Do research

Contents

Treasure Island

From **The Kettleship Pirates**

by Rodney Peppé

Down by the river lay an old kettle. Pip, Mary and Ma came to this spot each day to read *Treasure Island*. It was all about pirates and buried treasure.

When it was Pip's birthday, Ma knitted him a pirate cap and jersey. Pa made him a wooden cutlass.

1 What type of animal are Pip, Mary and Ma?

2 Write a few sentences to describe a pirate.

3 What did pirates do with their treasure? Why?

4 Draw a picture of a treasure box. What types of treasure are in your treasure box?

5 What is a cutlass? The picture of Pip might help.

Ma and Mary carried the birthday picnic. Pip ran on ahead to the river. In the old kettle's place he spied a pirate's hat! And just beyond it Pip saw the kettle. But it had turned into a pirate ship.

6 What were Mary, Ma and Pip about to do?

7 What do you normally use a kettle for?

8 Look at the picture of the kettleship. How did Pip know it was a pirate ship?

On board there were eight mice, and a rat with an eye-patch shouting orders. The rat pointed his telescope at Pip.

"I spy a spy!" he shrieked. "And he's stolen my captain's hat! Bring that thief aboard, mates."

9 Who was the rat with the eye-patch? How do you know?

10 How many animals were on board the kettleship?

11 Write a few sentences to describe the captain.
Begin each sentence with a capital letter and end it with a full stop.

12 What did the captain point? What is it for? Use a dictionary to find out.

The pirates were worried for Pip as he faced the captain.

"I didn't steal your hat, sir. I found it!"

"Bilge and barnacles!" roared Captain Rat. "You'll be cabin boy aboard this kettleship!"

Pip was taken below as the captain shouted to his crew, "Up anchor, mateys. We sail for treasure!"

13 Why were the pirates worried?

14 Use a dictionary to find the meaning of 'bilge' and 'barnacles'.

15 "We sail for treasure!" Write **five** sentences saying what will happen next.

Find the treasure

Let's have some fun and try to find the treasure by using **clues**.

The shaded start square on the map is found along line **B** and down line **2**. **You start at B2.** Make a list of the things that you pass to collect the treasure. The path you follow is: **D2, D4, C6, G7, H5, F3, E4,** and **E6.** DON'T FORGET to write down your list.

The Jolly Roger flag is in square **B1**. Write down the letters and numbers of this list of objects: **the pirate hat, the cutlass, the pistol, the parrot, the kettle, the cannon,** and **Pip.** REMEMBER – the **letter** comes first and the **number** last.

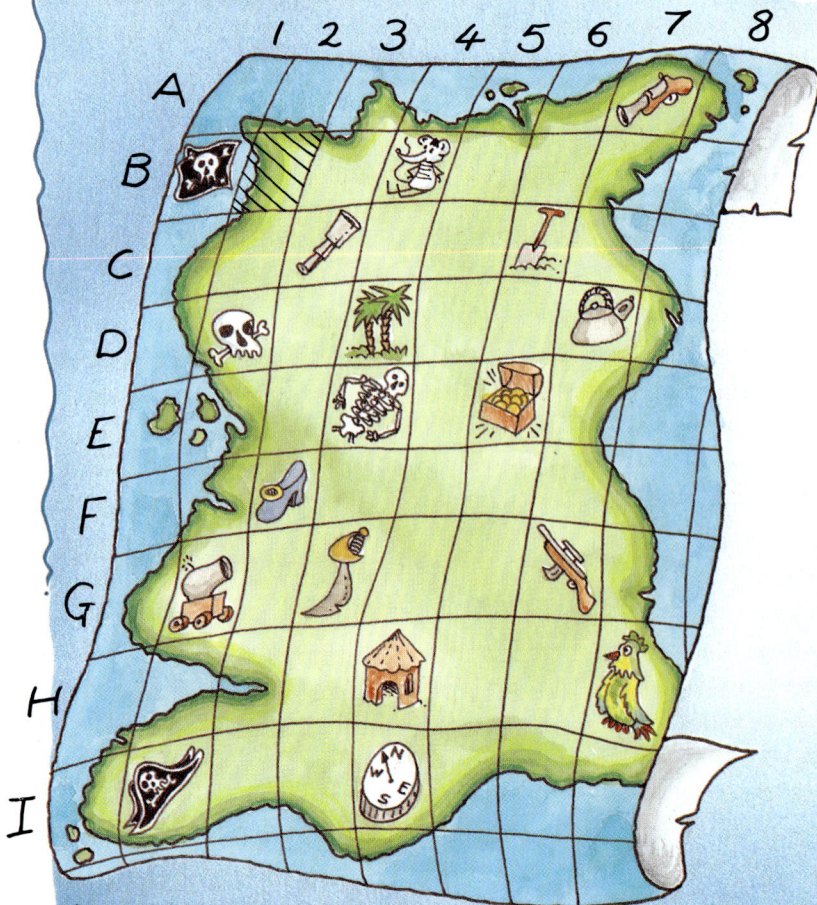

Draw your own **treasure island**.

Cover your island with squares. Put letters down the side. Put numbers across the top. Draw objects in some of the squares. Choose a square for your treasure.

Now make some clues to help your friends find the **treasure.**

You could use letters and numbers or objects. For example: What is in B2? Which square has the compass?

Ahoy mateys!

Let's design a **pirate's hat**.
But REMEMBER:

a   Write down how you will make it and the things you will use.

b   Draw a plan of the size and shape of your hat.

c   Now begin to make your hat.

d   When you have finished, write a few sentences to say how it turned out.

Jolly Jack

Jolly Jack the p_____

In his evil captain's h___ ,

Set sail to look for t_____

After looking at the m___ .

He waved around his c_____

Shouting, "Follow if you dare!

Let's land upon the i_____

And a promise we will swear.

That once we've fired the c_____

(And on this I must be frank),

If we capture any prisoners

We'll make them walk the p_____ ."

Find the words in the sails of the pirate ship to fill in the blanks. Then write out the poem.

How many pirates are hiding on the ship? Give them names. Choose one of the names and write a pirate poem. Try and make it funny. Draw a picture of your pirate.

7

The desert island

Look at the map. Jolly Jack has been left on the island. Can you get him off?

You can only sail through **empty** squares. Draw a line to show the way you will go. Write down the names of the squares. REMEMBER – the **letter** comes first and the **number** last!

Pirates decide to leave you on a desert island. You may take **five** things to help you. What will they be and why will you take them? Talk it over with a friend. Then do it like this:

1 I will take . . . . because. . . . .

The pirates allow you to take someone with you. Who will it be? Why would you take him or her? Do it like this:

The person I would like to take with me is . . . . because. . . . .

Message in a bottle

To get off the island you put a message in a bottle and throw it into the sea. You hope someone will find it. Write down your message. Draw a map if it will help.

8

The Invaded Island

Time journey

Look at my time machine. It can go into the **future**. *It can go into the* **past**. *Today we are going back in time – into the past.* **Future** *and* **past**! *What do they mean? Look them up in a dictionary.*

We are going back to a time when people came to Britain from across the sea.

Look at the squares on our time journey. Find the answers to the clues in them. Write the answers in order. You will find they make a story. REMEMBER – all the answers are on this page.

TO THE FUTURE

TIME JOURNEY

Vikings began to attack in AD 793.

1017 and 1066?

What did the Vikings do?

What happened in AD 450?

The Romans left in...

What did Queen Boudicca do?

THIS WAY

Where did they come from?

What happened in 55 BC?

TO THE DINOSAURS

START HERE

A queen called Boudicca fought against the Romans in AD 61.

Saxons came and lived in Britain from AD 450.

The Normans came from France and won the Battle of Hastings in 1066.

Julius Caesar came to Britain with the Roman army in 55 BC.

The Romans left Britain in AD 410.

In 1017 the Vikings took over England.

Use the library

Find out about: **Julius Caesar, Queen Boudicca, King Alfred.** Write down what you find out.

The Romans came from Rome, in Italy.

Often when people invaded other lands they only went for a look around. People were frightened by the invaders and fought against them to keep them out. Here is a story about a lion who went where he didn't belong.

THE LION HOUSE

From **The Happy Lion**
by Louise Fatio

There was once a very happy lion. His home was not the hot and dangerous plains of Africa where hunters lie in wait with their guns; it was a lovely French town with brown tile roofs and grey shutters. The happy lion had a house in the town zoo, all for himself, with a large rock garden surrounded by a moat, in the middle of the park with flower beds and a bandstand.

Early every morning, Francois, the keeper's son, stopped on his way to school to say, "*Bonjour*, Happy Lion."

In the afternoons, Monsieur Dupont, the schoolmaster, stopped on his way home to say, "*Bonjour*, Happy Lion."

In the evenings, Madame Pinson, who knitted all day on the bench by the bandstand, never left without saying, "*Au Revoir*, Happy Lion."

Read the opening of the story. Now. . .

1   Draw **three** different pictures. Each picture should show where the lion lived and **one** of the people who came to visit him.

2   How do you think the lion came to be in a zoo?

3   Find the word 'bandstand'. Look at the picture, then write down what you think a bandstand is.

4   There are two French words in the passage, *'Bonjour'* and *'Au Revoir'*. What do you think they mean?

He *was* a happy lion. One morning, the happy lion found that his keeper had forgotten to close the door of his house.

"Hmm," he said, "I don't like that. Anyone may walk in."

"Oh well," he added on second thought, "maybe I will walk out myself and see my friends in town. It will be nice to return their visits."

5 Why do you think the lion was happy? (Remember what you read before.)

6 Who forgot to close the lion's door?

7 What do you think of the lion's plan to go into town?

Then the happy lion went into the cobblestone street where he met Monsieur Dupont just around the corner.

"*Bonjour*," he said, nodding in his polite lion way.

"Hoooooooohhh. . ." answered Monsieur Dupont, and fainted onto the pavement.

"What a silly way to say *Bonjour*," said the happy lion, and he padded along on his big soft paws.

"*Bonjour, Mesdames*," the happy lion said farther down the street when he saw three ladies he had known at the zoo.

"Huuuuuuuhhh. . ." cried the three ladies, and ran away as if an ogre were after them.

"I can't think," said the happy lion, "what makes them do that. They are always so polite at the zoo."

8 Write down what happened to Monsieur Dupont and the three ladies.

9 Why do you think they behaved like that?

10 Can you find out what an 'ogre' is?

Hey! Where do you come from?

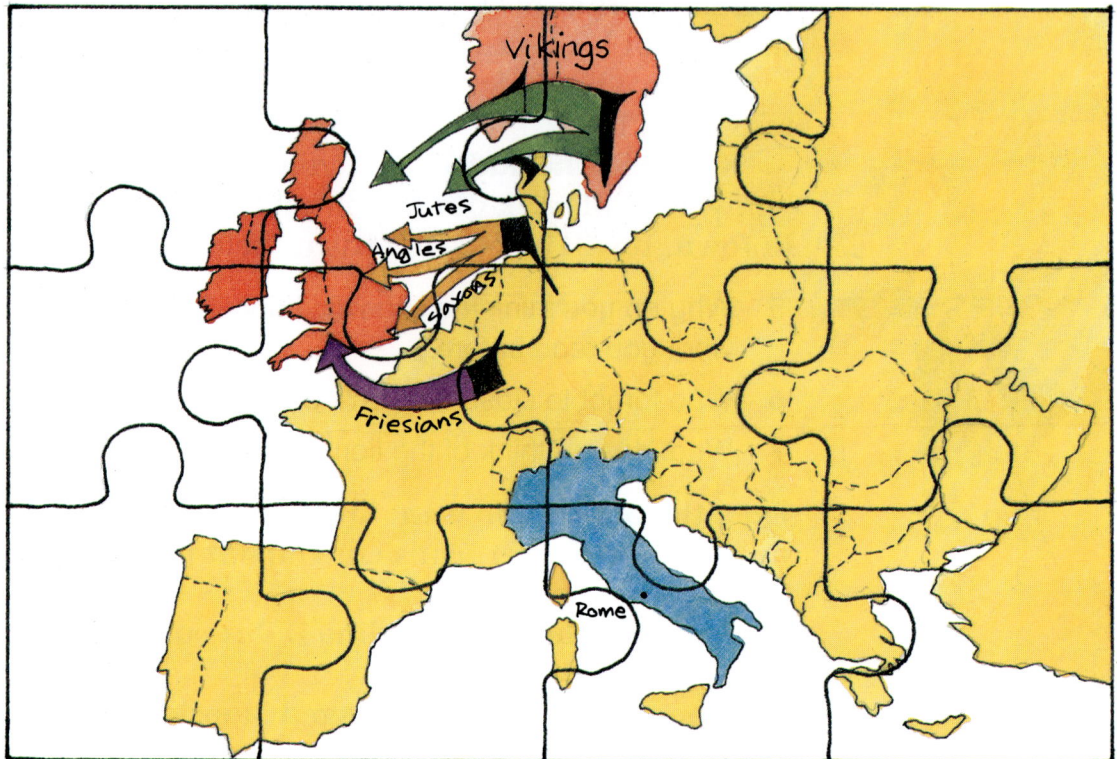

Here is a map showing where the Romans, Saxons and Vikings came from. There is only one clue. The map is called **Europe**. Find a book of maps, an **atlas**. You will need it to answer the questions.

Find a map of Europe in the atlas. Now let's do some map work. DON'T FORGET – write all your answers in **sentences**.

a   Look at the **red** shapes on our map above. Look at the map in your atlas and write down the names of the countries in the red shapes.

b   Which modern country did the **Saxons**, **Angles**, **Jutes** and **Friesians** come from?

c   What is the name of the country marked on our map in **blue**?

d   Which city do you think the Romans came from?

e   If the Romans had sailed to Britain, which **seas** would they have sailed across? **Look in the atlas.**

f The Vikings came from **S**_____ , **N**_____ and **D**_____ .

g On our holidays we **invade** other countries for a short while. Look at the map in your atlas. Write down the names of some of the places we might visit.

h **Here's a test**! Trace our map on the opposite page. Then cut out the jigsaw shapes and scramble them up. Now do the jigsaw and time how long it takes. Do it a few times and see if you get quicker.

When you have finished, stick the shapes on to paper and write in as many names of countries as you can.

Make a Viking longship!

You will need:
• *Squared paper* • *A lolly stick or cocktail stick* • *Glue* • *A matchbox*

1 Draw these shapes on squared paper. Cut them out.

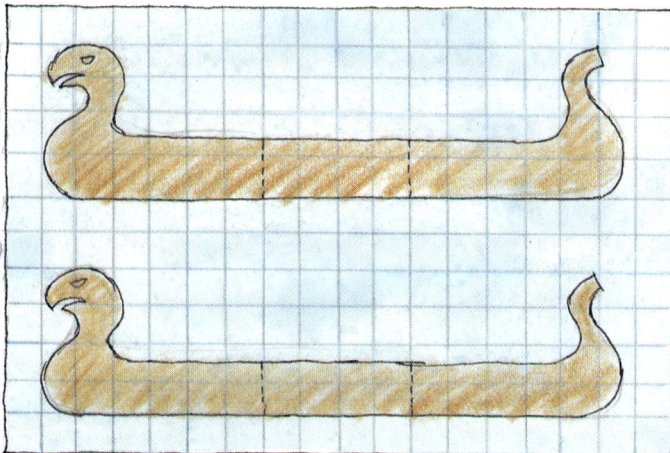

2 Use the matchbox to make this!

Glue both shapes to the matchbox.

3 Glue both fronts together and both backs together.

4 Make a paper sail. Then put the stick through the sail and into the matchbox.

Now decorate your ship.

They came in the night

Through the mist came the creak of many oars. Now and then there was a splash. The grey mist swirled and slid over the flat, grey sea, but not a sign could be seen of the boats; only the steady slap of oars and a few low curses.

   Then a dark shadow moved within the mist, growing blacker as it came nearer, until the great wooden hulk of a *Viking* war-boat emerged, trailing wisps of fog along its sides. Twenty oars bit into the water, and forty *Viking* warriors strained over the heavy poles.

*This is the beginning of a story about some invaders. Let's see if you can write one! But first of all, who were these invaders? Look at the words in **italics** in the story and look at the **picture**. Now give your story a **title** because:*

The raiders were about to attack a strange land. . .
Write **four sentences** telling how these men must have felt.

Soon the ship would slide to the shore. . .
Now write a **few sentences** about what will happen next. Why did they come? Where will they go? What will they do?

Finish the story by telling what will happen to the people who have been invaded, the Vikings and the great war boat.

Use a computer When you have finished your story:
a **Read it** and **check it** yourself.   b **Type** your story into the computer.   c **Keep checking** your story as you type it in.
d Using the computer **put right any mistakes** that you have made.
e When you have finished, **print it out**.   f Then **draw some pictures** for your story and make it into a book for another class.

War and weapons

When invaders came to Britain they had to fight very hard so that they could be in charge of the land. People used weapons to fight. All the different peoples had different weapons and wore different clothes. Before the Romans came, the Celts or the Ancient Britons lived in Britain. They looked like this:

The Ancient Britons had made farms and settled to keeping animals and farming. They often lived in hill forts. Some people lived in small villages around the hill forts. They grew wheat, barley, turnips, cabbages, beans and parsnips.

The Ancient Britons also liked to fight. They often used hand weapons but also used chariots, just like the Romans.

Look at the two pictures below. Now write **five** sentences for each of the pictures. DON'T FORGET to say who is fighting who!

Make a list with **three** headings showing the weapons used by: the Romans, the Vikings, and the Saxons.

Find **three** weapons in the pictures that begin with 's'. Write them down and draw them.

Hey! What are you doing here?

The Romans came from Rome, in Italy. They invaded many lands. Julius Caesar was the first Roman to come to Britain. The Romans knew that Britain was a rich country because it had tin, iron and copper. The people grew good crops. The Romans wanted more land.

After the Romans left, the Saxons came to Britain from Germany. The Saxons were made up of four different peoples: the Saxons, the Angles, the Jutes and the Friesians. It was hard to grow food in their own lands. Britain had good food and good land. At first only a few Saxons lived in Britain but later many more came.

The Vikings lived in Norway, Sweden and Denmark. Their lands were cold with deep rivers and high mountains. The Vikings did not have enough land to grow food or to have farms. They set out in their longships to seek land, food and riches using their skills as sailors and fighters.

*Now let's do some **research**. 'Research' means finding things out. The answers to all the questions below are on these two pages.*

Do research

1   Write two sentences saying why the Romans came to Britain.

2   Why did the Romans think Britain was a rich country?

3   Write down what you think would happen if your town was invaded by many strangers.

4   Find the names of the four different peoples who were the Saxons. DON'T FORGET to write your answer in a sentence.

5   Why did the Saxons come to Britain?

6   Write down why you think many more Saxons came to Britain.

7   Where did the Vikings come from?

8   Write down some words that tell us about the Viking lands.

9   What did the Vikings set out to find?

10 Pretend you are either a Roman, a Saxon or a Viking. You can be a sailor or a soldier. Write about an adventure that happens to you while invading Britain. Use some pictures from this book.

The Happy Lion

How the story ends. . .

All of a sudden a big red fire engine burst out of a side street, and came to a stop not too, too far from the lion. Then a big van came backing up on the other side of him with its back doors wide open.

The lion just sat down very quietly, for he did not want to miss what was going to happen.

The firemen got off the fire engine and advanced very, very slowly towards the lion, pulling their big fire hose along. Very slowly they came closer. . . and closer. . . and the fire hose crawled on like a long snake, longer and longer. . .

SUDDENLY, behind the lion, a little voice cried, "*Bonjour*, Happy Lion." It was François, the keeper's son, on his way home from school! He had seen the lion and had come running to him. The happy lion was so VERY HAPPY to meet a friend who did not run and who said '*Bonjour*' that he forgot all about the firemen.

And he never found out what they were going to do, because François put his hand on the lion's great mane and said, "Let's walk back to the park together." "Yes, let's," purred the happy lion.

So François and the happy lion walked back to the zoo. The firemen followed behind in the fire engine, and the people on the balconies and in the high windows shouted at last, "*BONJOUR!* HAPPY LION!"

11 Why do you think the fire engine came?

12 Did the lion know why the fire engine had come?

13 In your own words, write three sentences describing what the firemen did.

14 Who was pleased to see the lion?

15 Why were all the people happy at the end?

16 Write down all the words in CAPITAL LETTERS. Why do you think they are written this way?

Cars and Trains and Boats and Planes

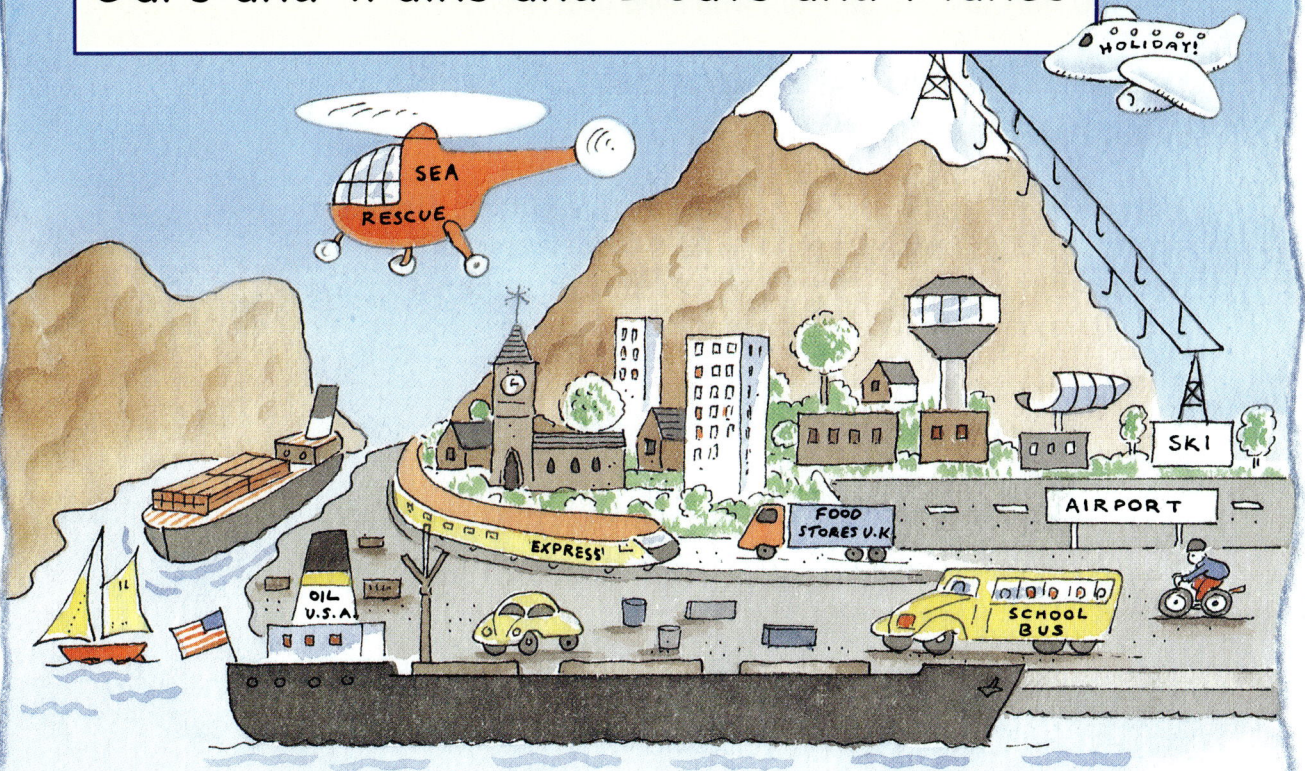

Look at the **picture**. It shows a very busy town next to a river and by the sea. The town is at the bottom of a snowy mountain.

a   Make a list of all the things in the picture that move.

b   Write one sentence for each thing. Say what it is doing. **Do it like this**: The barge is carrying timber to the busy town.

c   Draw a picture of your favourite type of transport. Say why you like it best.

Now do these:

d   Draw a road and then draw on it **four** things that travel on roads.

e   Think of **three** ways to get across a river. Write them down and draw them.

Here is a story about a little girl who lived by a river. . .

From **Birdy and the Ghosties**
by Jill Paton Walsh

There was once a little girl called Bird Janet, or Birdy for short. She lived with Papajack, her father, and Mamalucy, her mother, in a cottage where three things met. These three things were a road, a river, and the sea.

1 Read the beginning of the story again. Make **two** lists:
   a Write down the **names** of the people who lived in the cottage.

   b Write down the **three** things that met at the cottage.

2 Choose **one** of your lists and draw and label a picture about it.

Papajack had a stout little boat, called *Grey Goose*, and he worked as a ferryman, rowing people across the river, and saving them a long walk inland to the bridge upstream.

3 Why did people use the ferry?

4 Copy the picture of the boat. Write the boat's name underneath. DON'T FORGET to use a capital letter at the beginning of each word.

Birdy was too little to help much, but she did her best to be useful to her mother, milking the goat when she got up in the morning, and gathering the rough-shelled dark mussels that clung to the rocks on the sea-shore, to help fill the supper pot on the range.

5 Describe **one** way that Birdy helped her mother.

6 Find out what a 'mussel' is. Write it down.

Off on our holidays

Each year most of us go on holiday.
Some of us go for days.
Some of us go for weeks.
Some of us go for fortnights.
But how do we get there?

What type of transport do people use to go on holiday? Ask all your classmates how they travelled to their holiday.

Collect the information like this:

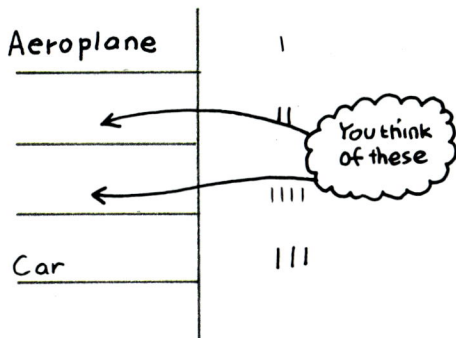

Aeroplane | I

You think of these

II

IIII

Car | III

Then use the information to **draw a graph** like this:

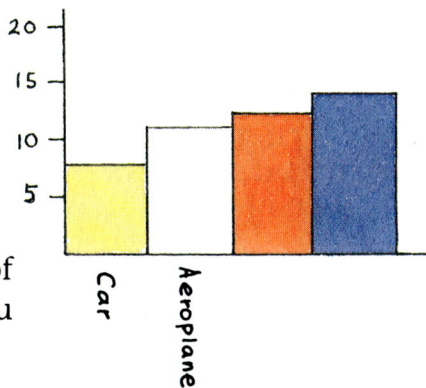

20
15
10
5

Car   Aeroplane

Which was the most popular way of travelling to a holiday? Why do you think this was the most popular?

How are these people going to get to their holiday?

Airport   Taxi   Railway Station   Bus stop

CYPRUS   Blackpool   Scotland   London   Florida

Write a sentence for each one. Begin like this:

The man in the blue suit will take a. . . . . to. . . . .

21

Story Start

The Ice-Cream Bandit

Once upon a very long time ago, when children were polite and teddy bears had picnics, there were two brothers and a sister. They came from Italy – their names were Guiseppe, Frederico and Maria.

They ran an ice-cream shop on the edge of the great forest. Each year Guiseppe, Frederico and Maria were in charge of the Teddy Bears' Picnic. It was their job to make the ice-cream.

Early one morning, long before the birds sing and just before the sun smiles, Maria heard a strange noise downstairs in the shop. Maria was very brave! She went to investigate. The shop door was open! The ice-cream tub was empty! Every lick of every ice-cream was gone – VANISHED!

"Guiseppe!, Frederico!" screamed Maria.

"We've been burgered! No, burgled! Someone's PINCHED the ice-cream!"

Guiseppe and Frederico shot down the stairs. All three dashed into the clearing at the edge of the great forest. The ice-cream trail disappeared into the darkness of the forest.

"What on earth shall we do?" asked Maria.

"Only two days to the Teddy Bears' Picnic!" cried Guiseppe.

"They'll be so disappointed," wept Frederico.

Guiseppe looked at Maria, Maria looked at Frederico and Frederico looked at Guiseppe.

"Only one thing we can do!" shouted Guiseppe, because he was the oldest. "INTO THE FOREST! AFTER HIM!"

ONLY two days to the picnic!

WHAT is going to happen to Guiseppe, Frederico and Maria in the deep dark forest?

WHAT adventures are in front of them?

WILL they get the ice-cream back in time?

AND REMEMBER THIS:
In the forest they meet a . . .
FIRE-BREATHING DRAGON

and a SEVEN-HEADED MONSTER

and GEORGIO!

Read the beginning of the story again. **Now finish the story. Draw pictures as well.**

(DON'T FORGET the dragon, the monster and Georgio.)

Chips with Everything

Here are some of our favourite foods and we like them all with chips:

Chicken and Chips

Chicken and chips,
Chicken and chips,
Everyone here likes chicken and chips.
  We eat them all day
  Never throw them away
We all like chicken and chips.

Choc ice and chips,
Choc ice and chips,
Everyone here likes choc ice and chips.
  We eat them all day
  Never throw them away
We all like choc ice and chips.

Chop suey and chips,
Chop suey and chips,
Everyone here likes chop suey and chips.
  We eat them all day
  Never throw them away
We all like chop suey and chips.

Chips and chips,
Chips and chips,
Everyone here likes chips and chips.
  We eat them all day
  Never throw them away
We all like chips and chips.

1 Read the poem to yourself **two or three times**.

2 Choose the verse you like best! Draw a picture of the food in the verse. Label the food carefully.

3 The poem is such fun to read because so many words have the same sound at the beginning – the '**ch**' sound. List all the words beginning with 'ch'.

4 Think of something you like to eat with chips. Can you write a verse about it like those in the poem?

Our favourite foods

Ask your classmates what they had for tea yesterday. **Collect the information** like this:

Chips ЖЖ ЖЖ ЖЖ IIII (= 19)
Beefburgers ЖЖ I (= 6)
Pizza IIII (= 4)
Sandwiches III (= 3)
Ice-cream ЖЖ IIII (= 9)
Fishfingers ЖЖ III (= 8)

When you have collected the information, **draw a graph** like this:

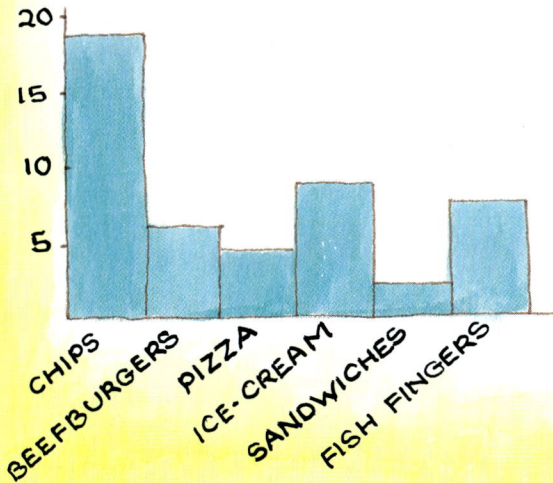

Write down the most popular tea-time food.

Write down the most unpopular food.

Write down everything you had for tea yesterday.

Now ask your classmates what their **favourite** food is! **Collect the information** as you did before and **draw** your graph.

What was the favourite food? Why did your friends choose theirs? Write down **five** of their reasons.

A world without chips

Can you imagine a world without chips? If it hadn't been for a famous Englishman, **Sir Walter Raleigh**, we wouldn't be able to have chips with everything! This is what we know about him – **the facts**.

He lived more than four hundred years ago.

His queen was called Elizabeth, like our queen.

He sailed on many voyages looking for gold and treasure.

He went to America and saw many plants.

He helped people bring potatoes across the sea from America to England.

The potato grew well in England.

People learned to cook them.

Potatoes became an important food for the poor.

We still eat potatoes today.

Sometimes potatoes are cut into sticks and fried in fat or oil – chips!

Write down **three** facts you have read about Sir Walter Raleigh. Then in your own words write 'The history of the chip'. There are lots of things on this page to help you.

Poor Walter!

Sir Walter Raleigh brought potatoes to England but he never tasted a chip and he never went to a fish and chip shop. But look at what he started. . .

Let's pretend we have just opened a fish and chip take-away called **'Sir Walter's'**.

The first thing we need is a **menu** to tell people what we sell and how much each item costs. Make the menu but DON'T FORGET the **prices**. There are 10 things on the menu.

MENU

cod	£1·20
chips	50p
sausage	40p
chicken	£1·30
haddock	£1·10
pickled onion	20p
pasty	70p
beef pie	80p
fish cake	60p
spare ribs	£1·00

How many different meals can I have for under £2.00? It **must** be a meal with chips.

How much **change** will I get from £2.00? Do it like this:

cod	£1·20
chips	+ 50p
	£1·70
	£2·00
	−£1·70
change	30p

The potato came all the way from **America**. The Native Americans gave it to Sir Walter Raleigh. It must have been a great adventure.

Pretend you are Sir Walter Raleigh and write a story about your exciting adventure to America. Think about: **a** The ship **b** The crew **c** The journey **d** Landing in America **e** The Native Americans **f** The journey home **g** What people thought about the potato.

Read your story again and put it right. Look at the sentences and the spelling and then copy it out in your best writing. **Now show your teacher.**

27

Before the chip and before Sir Walter

A very long time ago people found their food by hunting. They didn't keep cows, pigs and sheep. They didn't grow wheat, fruit and vegetables in fields and gardens. They hunted animals, fish and birds. They also collected berries and plants – just like the person in the picture.

After a long time people began to settle in one place and began to **farm**.

Soon lots of farmers had:

a brown cow that gave plenty of rich creamy milk,
two white sheep that gave soft warm wool,
a fat pink pig with a curly tail,
a rooster that crowed in the morning,
a hen that laid a large brown egg each day,
a dog to guard the house.

1   How many creatures did the farmer have?

2   Most of the creatures did something but one didn't do anything. Which one?

3   What was special about the wool?

4   Find **two** words that describe the milk. Write them down.

5   Write down all the colours mentioned in the passage.

6   Draw a picture of the farmyard. Put in all the animals and DON'T FORGET Mr. and Mrs. Farmer!

Farming today

For thousands of years farming was very simple. People used tools such as a basic plough, a scythe and a sickle. Look at them in the picture. Once modern machines had been invented, farming changed completely. On this page there are pictures of modern farm machines. You can see that they are pulled by tractors.

Look closely at the three pictures below. Write down what you think each machine does. Write **three** sentences for each picture.

Plough

Seed drill

Pick-up baler

Use the library

Find some books about farming. Look for the plough, the seed drill and the pick-up baler. Write down **in your own words** what they do.

Look at the picture of the combine harvester. Find out **three** things it does and write them down.

Draw a picture of the machine you like best and **label** its different parts.

Finally, who was **Jethro Tull?** Find out in the library!

Combine harvester

Farming research

The Normans (1066-1154)

After the Battle of Hastings in 1066 William the Conqueror shared out all the land of England. He gave it to his nobles and barons. The nobles shared some land with leaders in villages known as Lords of the Manor. Each person had someone in charge of them. The villager looked up to the Lord of the Manor, the Lord of the Manor looked up to the noble and the noble looked up to the king. This was known as the *feudal system*.

Look at the picture above. You can see the land is divided into strips.

Each villager was allowed to farm three strips. Each year the strips were changed round. One field would have oats or barley, the second would have beans or peas, the third was left to grow wild and the cattle would eat the grass.

The Middle Ages (1300-1485)

Look at the picture of a peasant's long-house. The poorest people lived in these houses about 700 years ago.

In the Middle Ages rich people ate lots of meat such as venison, rabbit, hare, goose, dove, partridge, grouse, moorhen, thrush, redwing and blue tit.

If the poor people ate meat it was usually beef or goose. They ate a lot of fish – cod, herring, haddock, plaice, whiting and mackerel. The fish was smoked or salted to make it last longer.

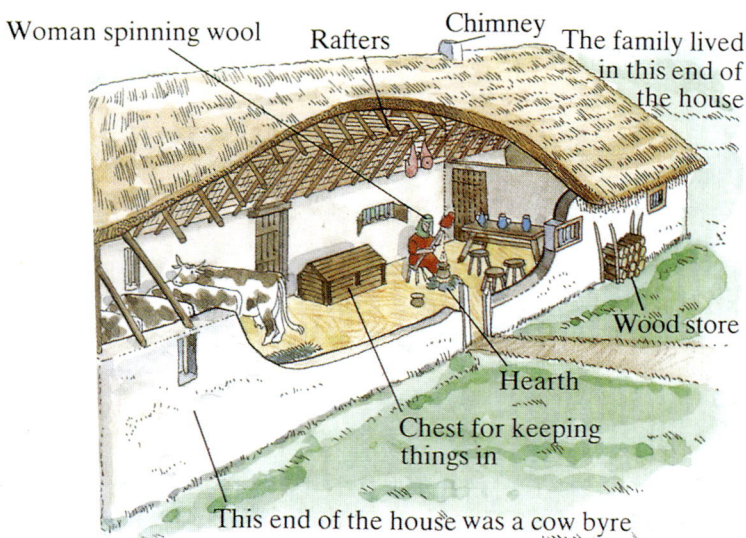

Woman spinning wool
Rafters
Chimney
The family lived in this end of the house
Wood store
Hearth
Chest for keeping things in
This end of the house was a cow byre

The Tudors (1485-1603)

About 500 years ago farming changed quite a lot. The rich people were called the gentry. They now used the land to grow and sell wood to build houses and ships. They also sold wool and corn. The rich people stopped the poor people farming their strips by fencing off the land.

Farmworkers and villagers now became very poor. They didn't own any land. Some of them were able to rent the land. Some worked and were paid wages. Even then some did not get paid in money but were paid in food. If crops were poor, many people starved.

Do research

1 Who do you think won the **Battle of Hastings**?

2 What were the leaders of villages called?

3 What did the villagers use the **three strips** of land for?

4 Why do you think the village in the picture is from **Norman** times?

5 Write **four** sentences about a **peasant's long-house**.

6 What did rich people eat in the **Middle Ages**?

7 How was food made to last longer?

8 Why do you think cows were kept inside houses in the Middle Ages?

9 In **Tudor** times what were the rich people called?

10 Make a list of the things that were sold in Tudor times.

11 What happened to **farmworkers** between 1485 and 1603?

12 What did the **rich** people do to the **poor** between 1485 and 1603?

The Victorian Times

6th July 1874   Price 2d.

It has been reported today that many towns are growing much larger because factories are giving people jobs. More people are living in the towns than in the country. Farms are growing food for the people in towns.

Farmworkers need a good crop of corn to make a living. If the harvest is bad, then poor people will starve. The wages paid by the farmer are already very low. All members of the family need to work on the farm. New machines that do jobs quicker mean that fewer people are needed to work on farms.

Many people are leaving the farms to look for jobs in towns. Some people are even leaving England altogether to live in different lands.

This story was in the newspaper on 6th July 1874. It tells us what is happening to the people who live on farms. **Let's look at the facts**. Write down **five** things that are **true** in the newspaper story. Write out the **complete sentences**.

The supermarket

*Today farms give us cereals, meat, vegetables, milk, cheese and eggs. Many factories make food. Nearly all the food we buy is sold in shops. The biggest type of shop is called a **supermarket**. We go to a supermarket nearly every week and pick our own groceries. We put them in a trolley and pay at the till.*

Look at the trolley in the picture. Now. . .

a **Get a calculator**. How much do all the groceries in the trolley cost?
b How much do the tins cost?
c How much do the packets cost?
d How much do the bottles cost?
e How much is the most expensive item?

32

Food, glorious food!

A long, long time ago nearly all our food came from our own country. Now we get food from all around the world. Almost everyone likes food from different countries.

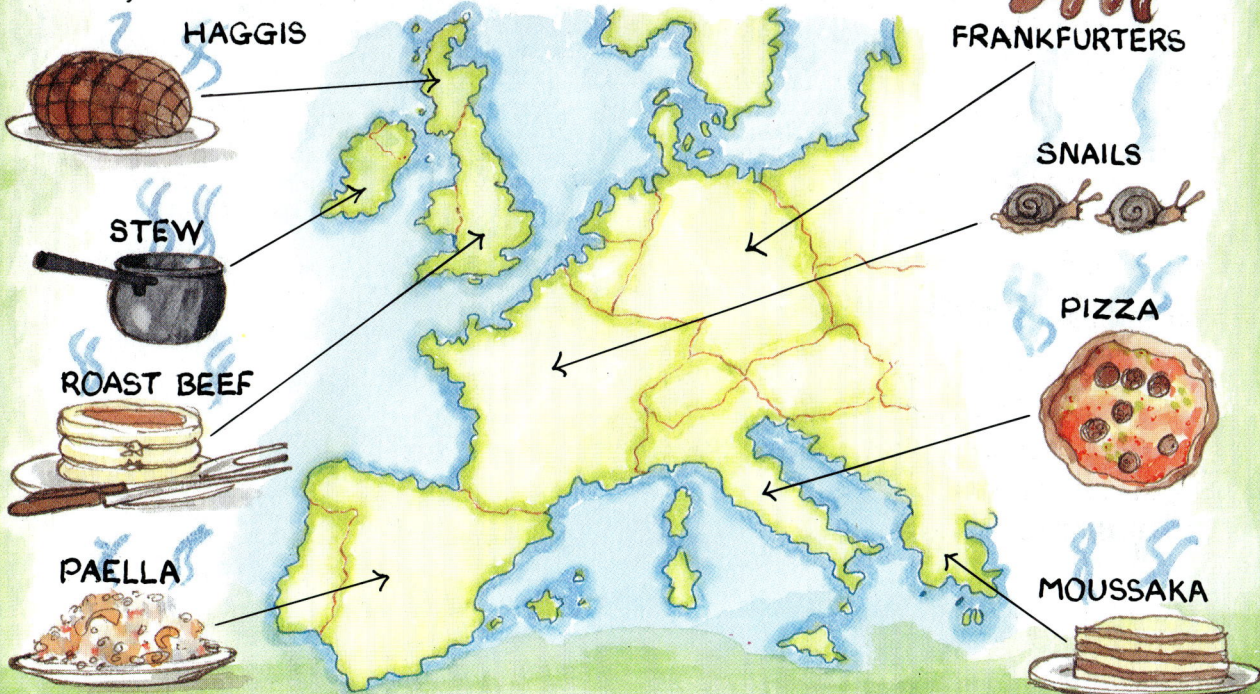

HAGGIS

FRANKFURTERS

SNAILS

STEW

PIZZA

ROAST BEEF

PAELLA

MOUSSAKA

This is a map of **Europe**. Instead of the names of countries you can see the names of different meals. **Here's what to do**:

a   Get an atlas.

b   Find a map of Europe.

c   Trace our map above.

d   Use your atlas to find out which countries the meals come from.

e   Write the name of each country on the map you have traced.

Use the library

Choose one country other than England and find out as much as you can about it. Then choose **six** of the meals on the map and look them up in a dictionary. Write down what you find out.

Thirsty food and cold chips!

*For thousands of years we have used fresh fruit and vegetables for food. But now we also have dried foods in packets. These foods are easy to use and can be stored for a long time. They have become **dehydrated**. All the water has been taken out of them. Let's give some of them a drink. . .*

Here's the experiment:

1 Take one teaspoonful of:
   - Dried onions
   - Porridge oats
   - Instant mashed potatoes
   - Dried mixed vegetables

2 Put each teaspoonful on a saucer.

   Add a small amount of water.

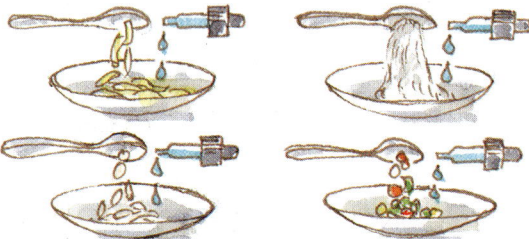

3 OBSERVE!
   Watch closely what happens to each saucer.

4 Now write down:
   a What you did.
   b What happened in the experiment.
   c Why you think this happened.

   Then draw pictures to help others to understand.

*Not only can we dry food – **we can also freeze it solid!** Frozen food keeps for many months. We can buy frozen food straight from a shop. And not just frozen chips!*

Make a list of foods that can go into a **freezer**. Write out the list in **alphabetical order** ('A' words first and 'Z' words last). The challenge is to write down **10** or more things.

Dustbins

Dustbins can be very interesting. People throw all kinds of things into dustbins. We can often learn things about people by looking into their bins and seeing what they throw away. But first here is a story about a little boy whose name was 'Dustbin Charlie'.

From **Dustbin Charlie**

by Ann Pilling

A visit to Grandad's

His real name was 'Timothy Charles Treadwell', but Grandad called him 'Dustbin Charlie'. This was because his very best thing was watching the rubbish men with their yellow lorry. They stopped at each house, picked up the dustbin and emptied it into a special grinder. Then the grinder chewed everything up with a great clanking noise. Grandad lived in a house on Union Street. . .

1 Copy the picture of Charlie. Write his real name underneath. REMEMBER to put a capital letter at the beginning of each word.

2 Write down the name Grandad called Charlie. Why did he call him this?

3 Where did Grandad live?

4 What did the grinder do?

5 What goes into your dustbin at home? Write down as many things as you can think of.

35

Where did Charlie live?

They didn't have dustbins at Charlie's – he lived on a farm in the country. Their house was in a long, green valley with hills all round. They had two cats and three dogs, twenty hens and a hundred sheep. But there were no children to play with at all.

6 Where did Charlie live?

7 Why do you think they didn't have dustbins?

8 Where was Charlie's house?

   a Find out what a **valley** is – write it down. Draw a picture to help you.

   b Find out what a **hill** is – write it down. Draw a picture to help you.

9 Look at the list below. It's about Charlie's farm. Write the name and draw the picture for each number:

2

3

20

100

10 How do you think Charlie felt on his farm?

What a load of rubbish!

Look at this row of houses. Each house has its dustbin outside. I wonder if you can work out who lives there by looking at the things that have been thrown away?

Write a sentence saying who lives in each house. **Do it like this**: In Number One. . . Then make a list of the things in each person's bin.

There was a time when everything in this bin would have been thrown away on to a rubbish dump.

Let's empty the bin. **Write down** everything that is in the bin. Put the items in **alphabetical order**.

These days we do not throw everything away. Some things are **recycled.** They can be used again to make something else.

Write down all the things in the bin that can be recycled. Add to the list anything else you think of that can be recycled to be used again.

The Living Island

From **The Turtle and the Island**

by *Barbara Ker Wilson*

Long, long ago, in the days when *turtles* had teeth, there lived a great sea-turtle, the mother of all sea-turtles, who spent her time swimming about the wide *sea* that now people call the *Pacific Ocean*.

Sometimes the turtle grew tired of swimming, and rested just below the *surface* of the sea, but she often longed to rest in the warmth and sunshine. She thought how pleasant it would be if only there were a piece of land in the middle of the great ocean where she lived.

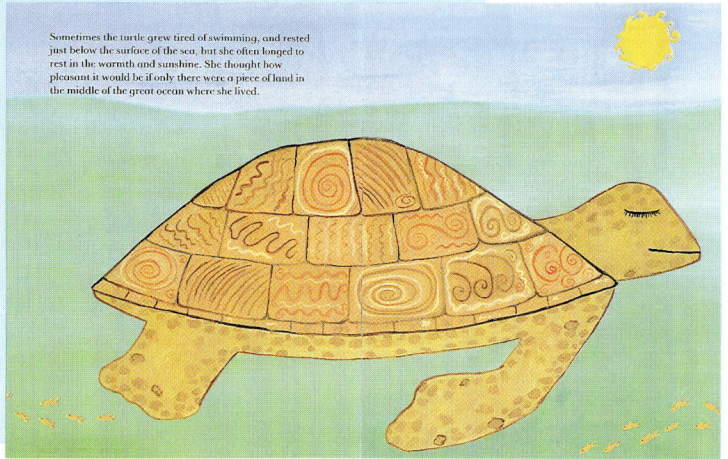

Sometimes the turtle grew tired of swimming, and rested just below the surface of the sea, but she often longed to rest in the warmth and sunshine. She thought how pleasant it would be if only there were a piece of land in the middle of the great ocean where she lived.

1   Look at the **picture** above. Write down what you see in it.

2   Read the **passage** above. Write down **four** sentences of your own about the turtle. The picture and the passage will help you. DON'T FORGET to use a **capital letter** at the beginning of each sentence and a **full stop** at the end.

3   What name do we use for the water where mother turtle swam? Write it down using a capital letter at the beginning of each word.

4   When the turtle got tired what did she do?

5   Draw a picture of what the turtle longed to find.

The turtle uses rocks and sand from the bottom of the sea and makes herself an island. She works hard and the little island grows.

The sun rose and set, the moon *waxed* and *waned* day after day, and still the hill grew higher. And at last it became a huge island in the middle of the sea, and the turtle saw that her work was finished.

Then the birds that flew across the ocean from land to land brought *seeds* of plants and trees and dropped them on the island. Grasses and flowering plants and tall trees sprang up, covering the rocks and sand. It was a beautiful, *fertile* island, surrounded by the sea which *teemed* with fishes large and small.

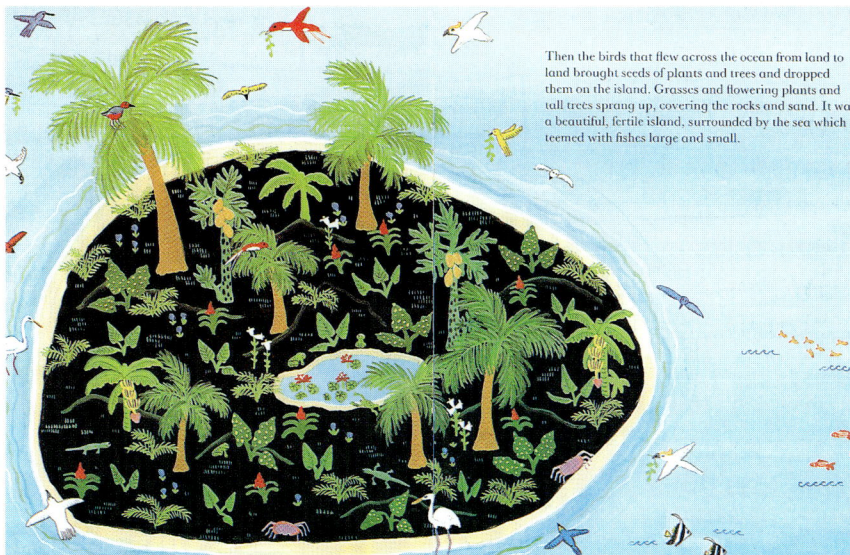

Then the birds that flew across the ocean from land to land brought seeds of plants and trees and dropped them on the island. Grasses and flowering plants and tall trees sprang up, covering the rocks and sand. It was a beautiful, fertile island, surrounded by the sea which teemed with fishes large and small.

6   Look at the picture above and read the passage again. **In your own words** write down how the turtle made herself an island. Write **four** or **five** sentences. DON'T FORGET capital letters and full stops. There are words in the passage that you can use.

7   How did trees and plants begin to grow?

8   If you lived on the island what would you eat?

9   How would you make a home?

10   Make a list of all the words in *italics* in the story. Look them up in a dictionary. Then write out each word and its meaning.

To grow and change

The turtle was helping to make the island grow and change. When the **Romans**, **Saxons** *and* **Vikings** *came to Britain they made things change. The things they* **did**, *the things they* **brought**, *the* **words** *they used all helped to make Britain different. They made the land* **grow and change**. *Let's look at some facts about them. . .*

Vikings built good ships and were good sailors.

Saxons wove clothes.

Saxons lived in villages and farmed.

Romans built straight roads.

Vikings traded things.

Rich Romans had central heating.

Vikings wove clothes.

Romans kept slaves.

Vikings visited many lands in their longships.

Romans built towns.

Saxons traded things.

Romans built forts.

Vikings farmed and lived in farmhouses.

Most Saxons were free but some were slaves.

Rich Saxons were called Earls or Thanes.

Use **three separate sheets of paper**. Put **one** heading on **each sheet: Romans, Saxons, Vikings**. Then write down each of the sentences above under its correct heading.

Now choose **one** of your sheets of paper – **either** Romans, **or** Saxons **or** Vikings – and write out your information in a sensible order. This time **use your own words** and try not to repeat yourself.

The Turtle and the Island

The turtle is lonely. She finds a man at the bottom of the sea and takes him to the island she has made. The story ends. . .

The turtle brought a woman to the island. She became the man's wife. The man and the woman lived together on the island in happiness and peace. They laughed, they played in the sea, sometimes they quarrelled, but they never lost the joy in their hearts.

They made children together, beautiful children, and those children had more children, and in this way the island became filled with people, who grew crops and built houses and fished along the seashore.

And in time the island that the great sea-turtle had made became known as Papua New Guinea.

Read the **passage** again. Look at the **picture**. Think of the turtle. . .

Now write your own story about how the island was formed, and how plants and people came to it. REMEMBER: **a Plan** your story. **b Look** for words that you might need. Write them down. **c Think** about pictures for your story. **d Don't forget** that you can re-write your story as you go along. **e Keep reading** what you write to make sure other people can understand your story.

Farmers and farming

*Britain became filled with people who grew crops, built houses and fished along the seashore. The **Ancient Britons** were farmers. The **Saxons** and **Vikings** who came to Britain were great farmers. They lived off the **land** and fished in the **sea**.*

These three pictures show the Ancient Britons, the Saxons, and the Vikings working in or near their villages. Now:

a Write **four** sentences for each picture.

b Pick **one** item from each picture and draw it.

c **Find out** what types of food the **Saxons** grew.

The Ancient Britons

The Vikings

The Saxons

Did you know?

*The **Romans** brought and left us many things:*

Cabbages

poppies

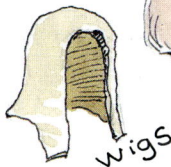
wigs

Carrots

Plums

Cherries

false teeth

roses

roof tiles

cats

nettles

pansies

peas

Use a **sentence** to answer each of these questions. DON'T FORGET to put a **capital letter** at the beginning and a **full stop** at the end. REMEMBER – your sentence must make **sense**!

a Which **animal** did the Romans bring to Britain?

b Write down three **vegetables** that the Romans brought.

c Draw pictures of three **flowers** that the Romans had and we still have today.

d Write down the name and draw a picture of something the Romans brought that you don't like. Write down why you don't like it.

e What are the oddest things the Romans brought? Why?

f Which items are the most useful? Why?

g Are there any things you would like to give back to them? Why?

h Which are the nicest things? Why are they the nicest?

Builders and warriors

The **Romans** had great armies. They had conquered Europe. When they came to Britain they brought lots of **new ideas**. The Romans began many things and some of them are still here today. There is lots of **evidence** to show that the Romans were in Britain.

Do research

A Roman villa

a What is a **villa**? Find out from a dictionary.

b Look at the picture below and make a list of the things that modern houses also have.

c How did Roman **central heating** work?

d Do you think rich or poor Romans lived in this villa? Give a reason for your answer.

e Write **four** or **five** sentences about the family that may have lived in this villa.

Chalk, sand and broken brick

Strong base shaped ston

Chalk and sand

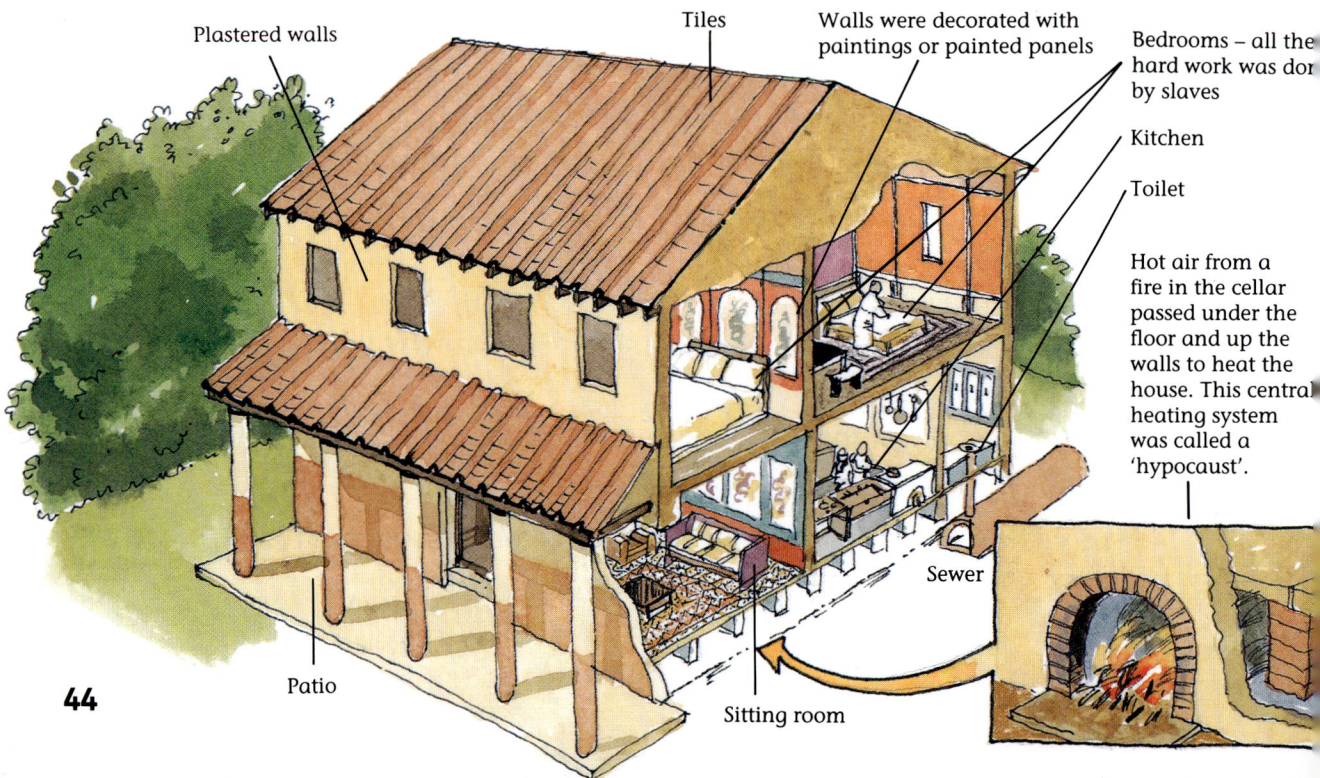

Plastered walls

Tiles

Walls were decorated with paintings or painted panels

Bedrooms – all the hard work was don by slaves

Kitchen

Toilet

Hot air from a fire in the cellar passed under the floor and up the walls to heat the house. This central heating system was called a 'hypocaust'.

Sewer

Patio

Sitting room

Do research   **Roads and walls**

f   Find out why the Romans built **Hadrian's wall**.

g   Make a list of the things that were used to build a **Roman road**.

h   What did sentries do on Hadrian's wall?

i   Look at the picture of the Roman road. Write some sentences saying how you think it was made.

j   What was a **milecastle**? What is a **turret**?

Ditch

Surface made from shaped, flat stones or gravel

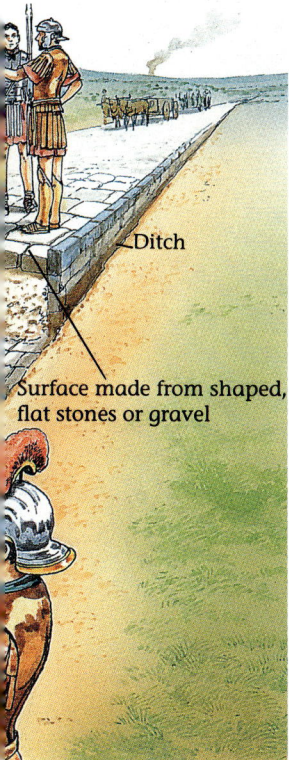

Now draw your own picture of Hadrian's wall and **label** it.

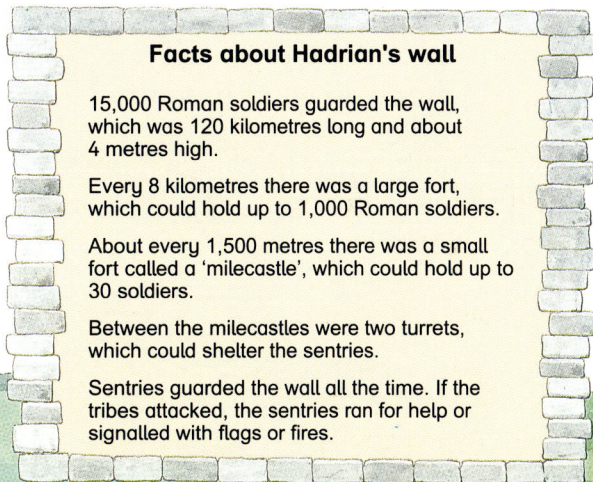

Hadrian's wall

Facts about Hadrian's wall

15,000 Roman soldiers guarded the wall, which was 120 kilometres long and about 4 metres high.

Every 8 kilometres there was a large fort, which could hold up to 1,000 Roman soldiers.

About every 1,500 metres there was a small fort called a 'milecastle', which could hold up to 30 soldiers.

Between the milecastles were two turrets, which could shelter the sentries.

Sentries guarded the wall all the time. If the tribes attacked, the sentries ran for help or signalled with flags or fires.

Milecastle

Turret

Be a Roman designer

*Romans often made pictures from **coloured** stones. They put these pictures on the floors of their buildings and houses. They called them **mosaics**. Many mosaics can still be seen today.*

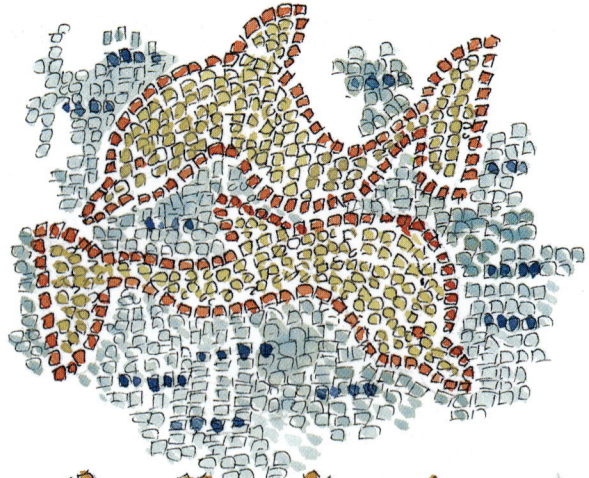

Design a mosaic!

1 Plan out and draw the picture you want in your mosaic.

2 Write down how you will make it and what materials you will use. (You can't use stones, you will need to have other ideas.)

3 Gather together the materials you need.

Then make your mosaic.

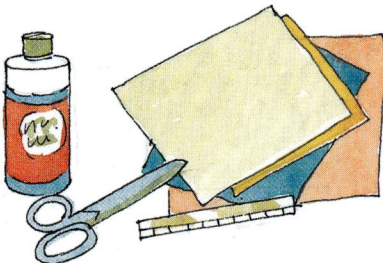

4 Write a few sentences saying whether the mosaic turned out as you had planned. If it didn't, how would you make it better next time?

Latin, German and Norse

In **England** most people speak **English**. But did you know that lots of English words are from different countries and languages? There are:

Roman words from **Italy,**
Saxon words from **Germany,**
Ancient British words from **Britain,**
Viking words from **Scandinavia,**
Scottish words from **Scotland,**
Irish words from **Ireland,**
Welsh words from **Wales.**

And the list goes on. All the words help to make up the English language that is spoken today.

But here's your chance to use a different language – **Viking** language. Look at the Viking **alphabet**:

a b c d e f g h ij k l m n o p

q r s t uvw X y z

Now write your friend a letter full of 'secret' messages in **Viking** language. Your friend will need to work out what it says and send you back an answer.

a Put your address at the top.

b Write in your friend's name (Dear_____).

c Write your message or letter.

d Put your name at the bottom.

DON'T FORGET – it must all be in **Viking**!

Poetry Corner

A poem by Jennifer Tweedie

Ocean Travel

If I could travel
the oceans blue,
these are the things
that I would do:

Fly with puffins
under the sea.
Dive with seagulls.
Fish for my tea.

Cling to the tail
of a rolling whale.
Leap with dolphins
in a buffeting gale.

Soar with an eagle.
Hunt with a shark.
Frolic with seals.
Fly home before dark.

a   Draw pictures for **one** verse of the poem. The
    pictures on this page will help.

b   Write down **five** creatures that are in the poem.

c   Write down the creatures in the poem that fly.

d   Write down the creatures in the poem that swim.

e   Copy out the poem in your **best writing**.

Rain, Hail or Shine

Here is a weather chart. It shows the weather over **one** week. The people who made the chart ticked the boxes **on each day** to show what the weather was like. Let's see if we can use this **weather information**.

	Sun	Cloud	Rain	Temp.	Wind speed	Wind direction
Monday	✓	✓		18°c	6	South
Tuesday		✓	✓	12°c	12	North East
Wednesday	✓	✓	✓	17°c	8	South West
Thursday	✓			21°c	2	South
Friday			✓	10°c	25	North

a   Write down the days on which it rained.

b   Look at the **wind speeds**. Write down the days in order – from fastest to slowest.

c   What time of the year does the chart show? Why?

d   Find out what a **compass** is. Draw one! Then mark on the wind directions.

e   Write a weather report for Wednesday.

Make a weather chart of your own – just like the one on this page. **Each day** you will need to tick the boxes and measure the **temperature**, the **wind speed**, and the **wind direction**.

How can you measure the **speed** and the **direction** of the wind? The pictures on this page might help.

REMEMBER – the **weather vane** points to where the wind is **blowing from**!

From The Weather Cat

by Helen Cresswell and Barbara Walker

One day a cat goes to live with a family. They call him Mr. Briggs. Naomi, the little girl, feeds and looks after him. She watches what he does! Let's go on. . .

If it was fine, Mr. Briggs would go and lie on top of the shed. He was looking for birds.

If it was fine but cold, he would lie inside the shed. He lay very still behind the sweeping brush. He was looking for mice and spiders.

But if it was wet, Mr. Briggs would soon come back into the house. He came in on tip-toe so as not to get his feet wet. Then he went into the cupboard under the stairs and slept all morning.

THEN NAOMI NOTICED SOMETHING ELSE. ON SOME DAYS MR. BRIGGS WOULD COME AND LIE IN HIS CUPBOARD EVEN WHEN IT WAS FINE. ON THE DAYS WHEN HE DID THAT, IT ALWAYS *DID* RAIN, LATER ON.

"Mr. Briggs is a weather cat!" Naomi told her mum one day. "He always knows when it's going to rain."

Mum was busy hanging out the washing. "It isn't going to rain today," she said.

"Yes it is," Otis told her. "Mr. Briggs is under the stairs."

Their mum laughed and went back inside. Not long after it began to rain. It poured. Everyone ran out to take in the washing.

"I told you!" Naomi cried. "Mr. Briggs is a weather cat!"

1 What did the cat do if it was not raining?

2 Why did the cat spend some time in the shed?

3 Write **three** sentences saying what Mr. Briggs did when it rained.

4 Read the lines in CAPITAL LETTERS. **In your own words** write down what Naomi has worked out about the cat.

5 Look at the writing in *italics*. How is Mr. Briggs trying to help Naomi's mother?

6 What do you think Naomi means when she calls Mr. Briggs a 'weather cat'?

7 How could a weather cat help you? Think about the things you do indoors and outside. You could draw pictures to go with your writing.

8 Draw **three weather signs** – one to show fine, one to show wet, and one to show cold. Then draw where the weather cat would be under each sign.

9 **Look up** the word 'weather' in a dictionary. See if you can find other things to do with weather in your class or library.

10 Write **three or four** sentences about weather – you can draw pictures as well if you want.

Here is the weather forecast

Each day we can hear the weather forecast on the radio. We can also watch it on television. The weather is important. It is very important if we are going on our holidays or out for the day. Here's your chance to make the forecast.

First let's look at these weather signs or symbols. . .

Cloudy

Cloudy with sunny spells

Showers

Snow

Rain

Stormy

Sunny

Wind direction and speed

Now. . .

TV. . . . .

1   **Trace** the **outline** of a map of the **British Isles** from an **atlas**.

2   Decide what the weather is going to be like. Choose your weather signs and draw them on to the map you have traced. Is it **winter** or **summer**? Don't get mixed up! Don't use too many signs. Make your map **colourful**.

3   Use the atlas to find a map of the British Isles with the **countries** marked on it.

4   You have to give the weather forecast on television tonight! So write your **script**, using the **country names** to show what is happening in different parts of the British Isles.

Poetry Corner

A poem by Moira Andrew

Calendar of Clothes

October brings scarves out again as leaves whirl up to the sky.

November means turned-up collars against wind and fog and storm.

May brings cotton tee-shirts with jumpers still on hand.

By June the skirts are skimpy, shorts short for playing on sand.

September, and it's back to school, uniform, shirt and stripey tie.

December shakes out party frocks. Christmas fun keeps everyone warm.

February likes hats with flaps and zipped-up coloured ski suits.

April needs a change of clothes for sun and wind and raindrops.

January is a time for coats, for caps and fur-lined boots.

March can do with anoraks and jeans and woolly tops.

August gets the sunsuits out with balls and buckets and spades.

July comes along in bathing trunks, and caps with dark green shades.

This poem seems to have got jumbled. It's all about clothes and the months of the year.

If the poem is put back together correctly it will rhyme. We know that **January** comes first, so write out the poem in the correct order. Do it in your **best writing**.

Draw pictures to show what is happening in January, June, July, September and December. That's **five** pictures altogether.

Seeds and Beans and Jack

Summer

Flowers grow from seeds, seeds come from flowers, flowers grow from seeds.

A *plant* has grown. It has a *flower*. In the middle of the flower there is a *seed box*. It contains many *seeds*.
In the *autumn* the flower dies. The wind shakes the plant and scatters the seeds on the ground.
The seeds are covered by the soil.

Winter

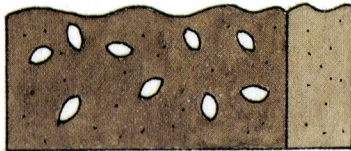

Summer

Spring

In the *spring* the sun shines on them and keeps them warm. It rains.

Hidden under the damp soil the seeds split. They open and start to grow. Slowly a plant grows up through the soil. It gets bigger and bigger. One day the plant grows a *bud*.

The bud opens and a flower appears. In the middle of the flower there is a seed box. It contains many seeds.

a Write down what happens in autumn, winter, spring, and summer. **Begin like this**: In the autumn. . .

b Draw **five** pictures to show what happens to the seeds from spring onwards.

c Write down the words in *italics*. Using some of these words, write your own story about a plant.

Use the library

d Find a book about flowers. See if you can name the parts of a flower.

Grow some seeds!

You will need:

- *A jar* • *Some blotting paper* • *Two bean seeds*

1 Take a piece of blotting paper and put it in a jar.

2 Place the bean seeds between the jar and the blotting paper.

3 Put about 2 cm of water in the jar and put it in a light and warm place.

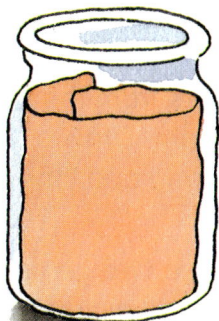

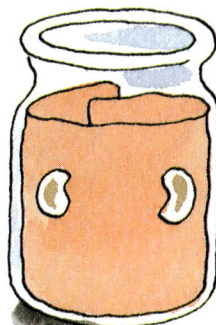

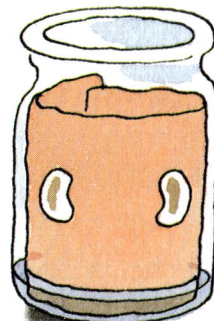

4 When the seeds begin to grow, measure the height of the shoot and the depth of the root like this:

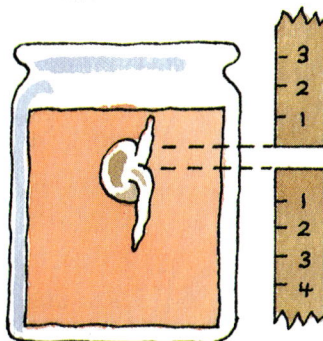

5 Make a diary to tell the story of your seeds. Each day write a short report of what is happening. Write your diary over two weeks.

From Class Three and the Beanstalk
by Martin Waddell

Miss Chew brought some 'growbags' so that the children in her class could grow things. Now read on. . .

Class Three spent the rest of the day talking about the growbags and the seeds they were going to bring. Miss Chew wrote up a list of their ideas on the blackboard.

"Bring your seeds to school on Monday!" said Miss Chew.

On Monday, everyone brought seeds in lunch boxes and bags and envelopes. Soon there were seeds all over the place. Pansies and cornflowers and rosemary and cress and peas and lettuce and radishes and forget-me-nots and marigolds and sweetpeas and beans.

1 Write down the things Class Three used to bring in their seeds. DON'T FORGET – begin each item on a new line.

2 Look at the list below. It's about the children's seeds. See if you can fill in the other letters.

be_____   pa_____

co_____   pe_____

cr _____   ro _____

fo _____   ra _____

le _____   sw _____

ma_____

3 Choose **two** flowers from the list. Find pictures of them. Draw the flowers, colouring and labelling them carefully.

4 From the list choose **two** items that you can eat. Find pictures of them. Draw the items, colouring and labelling them carefully.

5 Look at the list again. Find the word beginning 'ra_____'. Now write out the word. Use a **dictionary** to find out what kind of plant it is. Write down what you discover.

The story goes on. . .

Miss Chew picked up one of the packets.

"Jackson's Giant Beans," she said. "Who brought these?" Nobody seemed to know.

Class Three kept checking the growbags all day, but nothing happened.

"Wait and watch," said Miss Chew. "Seeds need a bit of time to grow, you know."

Nothing much happened for a couple of days.

Then, on Thursday morning, Class Three couldn't get into their classroom. The door was jammed.

They pushed and they pushed and they pushed.

6 Who brought the giant beans?

7 Draw a picture to go on the giant bean packet. Write the name of the seeds under your packet. DON'T FORGET to use a capital letter at the beginning of each word.

8 What did Miss Chew tell them about seeds? Use speech marks around her words.

9 Why do you think the children couldn't get into their classroom?

10 Look at the picture. Write down what you think is happening.
Try to write in sentences, as in the story. Use a capital letter at the beginning of each sentence and a full stop at the end.

Class Three and the Beanstalk

The story goes on again. . .

One moment the Class Three Beanstalk was coiling around the playground, finding new things to grow over, including cars and bicycles and people, with most of the school covered up in it. The next moment it gave a shiver and. . .

"H - E - L - P!" cried Miss Chew, as the leaf she was climbing off twitched upwards.

"Got you!" cried Kit. He reached out to grab Miss Chew's jacket and. . . WHOOOOSH!

The beanstalk shot off . . . and up and up and up and up . . . Till the top of it disappeared through the clouds. Miss Chew and Kit shot up with it.

"To the rescue!" cried Alice bravely and Alice and Class Three dived onto the beanstalk.

"HOLD THAT BEANSTALK DOWN!" cried Miss Grimthorpe. She didn't want the World's Biggest Beanstalk to escape from her school.

All the teachers and all the children (except Class Three) and all the dinner ladies and all the neighbours who had climbed over the school fence to help, tried to hold the beanstalk down but the beanstalk wouldn't stop.

Up and up and up and up it went. And up went Class Three with it.

11 Make a list of the things the beanstalk coiled round outside the classrooms.

12 Why did Miss Chew cry "H - E - L - P"?

13 Where was the beanstalk going?

14 Write in your own words how Class Three ended up on the beanstalk.

15 What did everyone else do after Miss Grimthorpe asked them to help?

Up in the clouds

Class Three and Miss Chew shot up through the clouds to the giant's world!

Write your own story about you and your classmates in '**The land of the giants**'. You might get some ideas from the picture on this page. DON'T FORGET to **draw pictures** for your story.

help!

Jack

Find the word 'giant' in a **thesaurus**. Write down more words that mean **giant**.

Crossword

All the answers are on this page.

Across
1   The giant's home (6)
4   He's at the top of the plant (5)
5   It warms the seeds (3)
6   The giant's name (4)

Down
1   Children of _____ Three (5)
2   You will find one on the plant (4)
3   The plant was a bean_____(5)

A giant grows taller and **taller** and **taller**

High, there!

by David Bateson

A girl next to us who's called Paula
Grew taller and taller and taller;
    When friends called out "Hi!"
    She kept wondering why
They looked **smaller** and smaller and smaller.

This little poem is called a **limerick**.
Limericks are often funny. The end words sound similar.
We say that they **rhyme** – like 'smaller' and 'taller'.

Try to write a funny limerick. Begin like this:
My best friend who is called . . .

Do we grow taller and taller just like Paula? Let's find out.

Find **one** person in **each class** in your school. Measure how tall each person is and measure the length of his or her feet.

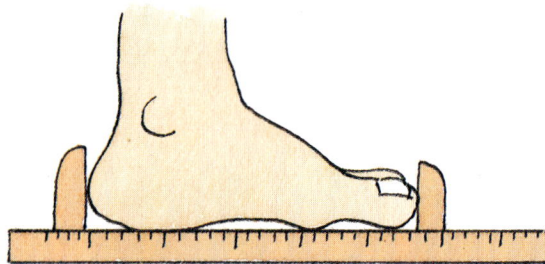

When you have done this, draw **two** graphs like these:

Under each graph write a few sentences explaining what it shows. Colour in your graphs.

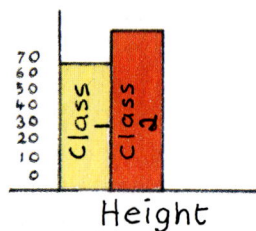

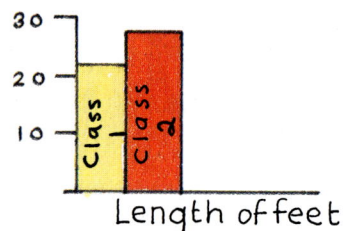

Good grub or bad grub

*Two things that help us grow are **healthy food** and **keeping fit**. The giant is going shopping for food. Let's look at his shopping list. . .*

chocolate apples
oranges milk
sugar frozen chips
sausages pop
eggs sweets
potatoes meat
fish cheese
carrots cabbage
butter hamburgers

Now make two lists:

a Write down the **healthy** food.
b Write down the **unhealthy** food.

Look at your lists. If you had to make the giant a **healthy** meal, what would you use? Draw a picture of the meal. Colour it in.

People and plants

People and plants are similar in some ways – people **breathe** and plants **breathe**, people need **food** and plants need **food**. But people and plants are also very different.

Look at the two pictures and write down what you know about trees and what you know about people. Write **five** things about each.

Oh dear, dear, dear!

The beanstalk has been growing for so long that everyone down below has forgotten about it.

The children, Miss Chew and the giant are still above the clouds. Animals have made their homes in the branches of the stalk – birds, dormice, squirrels, and the wise owl.

A farmer has come to chop down the beanstalk so that he can use the land for farming.

We must do something!

Write a **letter** to the farmer. Tell him all the reasons why he must not chop down the stalk. DON'T FORGET to put your address on the letter so that he knows where to write back.

If the farmer chops down the beanstalk, what will happen to the children? How will they get back down through the clouds to the ground?

Draw a picture showing how you would get them down.

Poetry Corner

Poems by Colin McNaughton

The Lion's Den

"Bring all your pets in tomorrow,
We'll all have a jolly nice time."
To teacher, a pet means a gerbil;
She obviously hasn't seen mine!

Who's Been Sleeping in My Porridge?

"Who's been sitting in my bed?"
said the mummy bear crossly.
"Who's been eating my chair?"
said the baby bear weepily.
"Who's been sleeping in my porridge?"
said the papa bear angrily.
"Wait a minute," said Goldilocks.
"Why can't you guys just stick
to the script? Now let's try
it again and this time no messing about."

Mum is Having a Baby!

Mum is having a baby!
I'm shocked! I'm all at sea!
What's she want another one for:
WHAT'S THE MATTER WITH ME!?

a   Draw a picture for each poem.

b   How do you think the teacher will feel when she sees the lion? What might she do?

c   The three bears have got a bit mixed up. Write out the poem again and this time put the story right!

d   Pick the poem you like best. Copy it out in your **best handwriting**!

First published in 1995 by:
Stanley Thornes (Publishers)Ltd
Ellenborough House
Wellington Street
CHELTENHAM GL50 1YD
England

A catalogue record for this book is available from the British Library.

ISBN 0 7487 2056 1

Edited by Annie Scothern
Illustrated by Ian Heard, George Hollingsworth, Isobelle Morgan-Giles, Frank James and Jacqui Thomas
Designed and typeset by StoreyBooks
Printed and bound in Hong Kong by Dah Hua Printing Co., Hong Kong

Acknowledgements

The authors and publishers are grateful to the following for permission to reproduce copyright material:

David Bateson for the poem 'High, there!'; David Higham Associates for the extracts from *There's a Viking in my Bed* by Jeremy Strong and *Birdy and the Ghosties* by Jill Paton Walsh; Frances Lincoln Ltd. for the extract from *The Turtle and the Island* by Barbara Ker Wilson and the illustrations by Frané Lessac; HarperCollins Publishers for the extract from *The Weather Cat* by Helen Cresswell and Barbara Walker; Jennifer Tweedie for the poem 'Ocean Travel'; Ladybird Books for the extract and illustrations of Hadrian's wall and a Roman road from *The Romans*; Longman Group for the extract from *Flowers* by Althea; Macmillan Publishing Company (US) for the extract from *The Little Wooden Farmer* by Alice Dalgliesh; Moira Andrew for the poem 'Calendar of Clothes'; Oxford University Press for the poem 'Chicken and Chips'; Penguin Group for the extracts from *Class Three and the Beanstalk* by Martin Waddell, *Dustbin Charlie* by Ann Pilling, *The Kettleship Pirates* by Rodney Peppé, and the illustrations from *The Kettleship Pirates*; Simon & Schuster Young Books for the extract and illustrations from *Birdy and the Ghosties*; Walker Books Ltd. for the poems 'The Lion's Den', 'Mum is Having a Baby!' and 'Who's Been Sleeping in my Porridge?' by Colin McNaughton; Wayland (Publishers) for the illustration of a peasant's long-house from *Medieval Britain*.

Every effort has been made to obtain permission prior to printing. However, this has not always been possible and the publishers apologise for any errors or omissions. These will be rectified at the earliest opportunity.